THE INHERI

William Ayot

William Ayot first worked in London's gaming industry while developing as a playwright and poet. Following a personal crisis, he studied poetry, story and ritual under a remarkable series of teachers and shamans. By the mid nineties he was facilitating groups in rehab centres, and leading initiatory Rites of Passage for men. As a co-founding director of Olivier Mythodrama, he worked to bring narrative, imagination and poetry to organisations and business schools around the world. After reducing his business commitments, he set up *On the Border*, a groundbreaking poetry initiative in South East Wales. This led to the realisation of a long-held dream, the formation of NaCOT, the UK's first dedicated centre for spoken poetry, storytelling, and oratory. William also designs and leads rituals and works as a leadership coach. He lives with his wife, Juliet Grayson, in a restored Monmouthshire Gentry House near Chepstow.

also by William Ayot

Poetry

Small Things that Matter

Theatre

Bengal Lancer
Shakespeare's Ear

THE INHERITANCE

William Ayot

PS AVALON
Glastonbury, England

First published in the U.K. in 2011 by PS Avalon

PS Avalon
Box 1865, Glastonbury
Somerset, BA6 8YR, U.K.
www.willparfitt.com

Design: Will Parfitt

Cover image – 'Quinces' – by Jenny Barron
Water colour – From the author's collection

Back cover photo: Castle Portraits

ISBN 978-0-9562162-5-0

CONTENTS

ACKNOWLEDGEMENTS

Some of these poems were first published
in the following publications:
*Achilles Heel, Acumen, Candelabrum,
Poetry London Newsletter, Psychopoetica,
Spokes, Still, Weyfarers,
The Making of Them (Lone Arrow Press),
Writing for Self-Discovery* (Element),
The Water-Cage (Sleeping Mountain)
and *Into the Further Reaches* (PS Avalon)

— To the Grandfathers —

THANKS

are due to the following artists, teachers,
practitioners and individuals who at various times
have given the author guidance, help or support:
Robert Bly, James Hillman, Martín Prechtel,
Lowijs Perquin, Malidoma Somé, Sobonfu Somé,
Shi Jing, Ron Pyatt, Richard Olivier, Steve Banks,
Mark Rylance, Geoff Mead, Jeremy King,
Paul Smith-Pickard, Robert Sherman,
Simon Powell, Myra Schneider, Paul Groves,
Jay Ramsey, John Hegley,
and Juliet Grayson Ayot.

I

BLOOD AND BONE

NEW YEAR'S EVE

Year's end, and the grief is with me,
unshed tears at the back of my throat
for those I failed, who didn't make it;
the ones who fell, who stumbled, reeling,
who would not, could not, make a change,
whose lives were lit by other stars
than those that shine so thinly now.

I will place a candle in my window —
not to guide them, still less to heal,
but to show them, wherever they are,
that I have kept faith, that I remember
their crooked smiles, their tipsy laughter,
heads thrown back in wild hilarity;
glasses raised, tall tales untold,
the dogs of disaster still on the leash;
dreams untarnished, dawns undimmed,
my foolish, frail, unforgettable dead.

HISTORY

I close my eyes, and imagine my parents
standing behind me, one at each shoulder;
behind them, and behind them, and behind them
two parents, travelling back in a vee through time.
Two, four, eight, sixteen, thirty-two, sixty-four —
in twenty generations I have a million ancestors.
I am the tip of an arrow. That's history.

I have a father in me, his frail heart breaking
on the battered anvil of his unlived life,
and a mother whose fear still trembles inside me,
reaching like a scold for the easy mask of anger.
They were good people. They made me who I am.
They left me ashamed of my body and my kind.

I have two grandfathers and two grandmothers,
on the one side dirt poor, on the other middle-class.
My grandfathers stare out of sepia photographs,
stiff in their uniforms like khaki butterflies,
chloroformed and pinned by the coming of war.
One granny died giving birth to my father,
the other endured, and drank herself to death.

I have war in me then, and the greed of Empire,
cruelties born of the ledger and the lash —
the boss's swagger, and the box-wallah's blag,
the foreman's snarl, and the slaver's dull-eyed stare.
I also have a pauper in me, driven from the fields,
grieving the memory of every pond and pasture.

There's a puritan in me who fought his brother,
and a Cavalier who wept as he buried his sons,
a whey-faced villager who pointed the finger,

tied his neighbour to a stake and watched her burn.
The neighbour's in me too, and she's not a witch;
and she did none harm, and she spoke none harm.

There's a monk, and a bishop, and a starveling curate,
and a hermit who went crazy alone in a cave;
each one giving their life to prayer and service,
each one stumbling on the unpaved road to God.
And there's a wet nurse too, and a silent midwife
who buried more children than she ever welcomed.

I've a troubadour inside me, and a crusader
prepared to do murders in the name of the Lord.
Their flags and their pennons flutter forlornly —
there's a bit of me that never got to Jerusalem.
Behind them there's a file of hard-faced warriors
and the sullen churls they ground into the mud.

There's a Celt, and a Pict, and a roaring berserker,
calling on the spirit of the Great White Bear;
and a völva in her trance, and a shaman drumming,
staving off the coming of hunger and pestilence.
These are my ancestors, my blood and my bone.
They make me who I am. I carry them with me.

ROMANTIC

Much thinner than he ought to be,
he begs no more than a smile or a blessing.

Head bent forward, shoulders hunched,
chapped hands deep in his empty pockets.

You could look into his flint-grey eyes
and see the stories of a thousand sons

brought to this city by hope or despair
at one last crop of thistles and stones.

You can hear him in the underpasses,
the delicate agonies of his dulcimer playing,

and all the while you can place him exactly
on the brow of a vast and motherly hill,

in silhouette against the skyline, a dreamer,
held down by nothing but the grasping clay.

THE INHERITANCE

This is the fear
my mother carried
like a cold, wet stone;
her rough hands cracked
with the handling of it,
her love worn thin
by its abrasions.

This is the fear
my father suppressed
like a squalling child;
his strong arms forcing
the pillow down on it,
tenderly, tenderly,
whispering a lullaby.

And this is the fear
I cannot own,
that I have wrapped
in the cloths of anger:
red for a warning
to keep me safe,
white for the grief
and the isolation.

This is the fear
of my generations,
handed down with
the bottle and the flask;
sharp as a cracked whip,
dull as a goad;
driving me, driving me
as they were driven.

FATHER AND DAUGHTER

(October, 1950)

A long black funeral car, nondescript as the age,
and you – austerity itself – in homburg and gloves
sitting with a tiny white coffin beside you,
stunned into silence by eight short days
of worry and gratitude, cruel choice and loss.

I'll take her myself, May. I can hear you say
though I was never there. *Better I do this alone.*

The scrunch of gravel, whispering conifers,
pity, and the doffing of hats and caps;
wreath-bearing visitors held by the sight of you
walking like a robot down the rows of graves,
holding out your offering, mechanised by death.

THE MADE BED

It would have been dark, or nearly dark,
and in the dark their loneliness would have been complete.
She would have waited beside him, listening to his breathing,
would have sensed his hand before it reached her,
might even have shrunk a little before it touched.
He would have whispered, like a beggar, abashed,
or the ghost of a child that has yet to let go. *Please.*
In the darkness she would have mouthed the word, *No,*
but as the hand took possession of her she would have sighed
and her body would have said, *Yes,* in spite of itself.
Neither of them would have been naked.
                                    The nightdress
he bought her would have been hoisted over her breasts
and his pyjama buttons would have scraped her skin
as he pulled himself on top of her. They would have kissed
through habit, the beer on his breath meeting the port on hers,
and, as the mattress began to creak and protest,
she would have heard her mother's querulous voice,
clear and distinct above the comedy of his breathing.
Well, you've made your bed, so you'd better lie in it.
Abruptly, her body would have flared and kindled.
She would have turned to him, peered at him, held his face.
For a second they would have been lovers again.
His need and her pity would have melted away,
would have dissolved into feeling, into clouds and light.
There would have been birds and a single cry
                        and then it would have been over.
Safe in the darkness she would have wept,
her lone grief bobbing on the swell of his snores,
while deep within her something would have quickened,
would have wriggled aggressively, demanded and joined;
then split, and split, and split again, both needed and unwanted.

A SUSSEX POEM

The years have all vanished like old Slindon Wood.
They lie shattered and broken, torn by the wind
While I, revisiting old familiar haunts,
Breathing rich downland air as I did of old,
Remember — Time makes tourists of us all.

Down off the hill with a church clock striking six,
A distant dog barking as if to test the stillness
And the scent of wood smoke, sweet apple and pear.
I was only passing through I know but in Sussex,
For a perfect moment, I belonged and was blessed.

Walking through woods in late October sunshine,
Beeches ablaze in restless glades of autumn gold,
Cherries already stripped of their dazzling brocade
And friends, kicking through the leaves, arm in arm,
Laughing — mocking the chill and the onset of the end.

Christmas Lunch and endless conversations
Spilling across the dunes and down to East Head.
Homeward like rooks across the pale December sky
To hot teas and presents and dogs by the fire.
Warmed through with love yet calling it company.

It's Christmas time once more. The years are long gone,
Gone with Belloc's plowman from Ha'nacker Hill.
Nothing is final. The windmill is turning again.
I am older, sadder. I can admit love now.
I knew it once in Sussex. They say I could return.

ANOTHER FUNERAL

Not the mourners with their drizzled faces,
nor the service with its dry embarrassments,
its gawky, shuffling infelicities,
nor yet the burial with its thud and wrench,
its dull flat, cauterising realisations —

but the involuntary halt by the cemetery gate,
the turn, the call, the sudden seeking
for the tiny grave hidden by the hedge,
a three-penny bit memorial, all but forgotten
yet found by that part in us that brings us home,
that listens to dreams and waits at thresholds,
reminding us of the might-have-beens,
the wraiths of our maybes, our lost potentials.

My sister the ghost-baby, unknown to me,
though she was a constant childhood presence,
a loss inexplicable, too huge for tears;
the hole in her heart a hole in our lives
that split us into assorted solitudes.

Now all our griefs come together in me:
renamed, acknowledged, mapped and followed:
each brook and stream, each tributary loss,
each laden, meandering river of bereavement.
We are heavy with the silt of our parents' tragedies,
un-grieved except in angers and busy-ness.
We are sluggish with them, ponderous, saturated.
My sister beckons me to weep down to the sea.

II

THE LAND OF GIANTS

WIRELESS

I am a radio station broadcasting to the world.
I am seven years old and I am sitting on a fence-post
overlooking the storm-field and the village beyond.

Being a radio station's more fun than being a train.
I was a train for ages: an express, then a sleeper,
then a goods, and then an angry little shunter.

Nobody speaks to trains because they're too busy.
But now I am a radio station, transmitting daily
to the far horizon — which is miles.

It's a varied programme including music, religion
and talks, and remembered bits of *Round the Horne*
that I take in on my crystal set before I fall asleep.

Every ten minutes I recite the news — What Miss Sims
said to my mum and how Dolly Feaver the postmistress
is still beating Pickles with a stick — which is cruel.

Sometimes I run out of news and then I sing things.
My song becomes a naming and my naming is a world:
Robin Hood and Little John and a pair of long trousers,

and Brock's Wood and the Hill and someone to talk to,
and the cedar and the elder and the elm and the oaks,
and the silver-backed mole and the pheasant and the lark,

and the weasel that steals the pheasant's eggs,
and the rooks and the rabbits, and nettles and docks
and the storm on the corn, and the clouds, and God....

COUNTING THE MARIGOLDS

The fist came out of nowhere.

He was nine years old and running up the garden path,
excited as only a boy can be
when he sees his father coming home.

Daddy, Daddy. I scored a goal!

It caught him right on the button.
Something split and he could taste the metal in his blood
before he hit the ground.

He was staring at a bed of marigolds,
concentrating, counting leaves and petals,
when his father picked him up and looked him in the eye.

I must have told you a dozen times, he slurred.
Never leave yourself open.

THE DELIVERY

The kilderkins lying in the cool of the cellar
manhandled, racked up, waiting to be drawn,
dumped off the dray on a rope pad, grabbed
and spun by expert hands. Billy Christmas
and his draymen calling out, '*ware below*,
and my father waiting as the barrels tumbled in,
upending them, grunting them into place,
smiling at the achievement, holding a mallet
ready to check the bung, to broach and tap.
Heavy tubs those barrels, eighteen gallons,
with every now and then a heavier thirty-six,
sitting there foaming through their wooden spiles,
the dank cellar cradling them, the delicious
cool of them, waiting on a hot September day.

And outside, Harry, cutting nettles in the orchard,
his one tooth beaming as he sharpened the scythe,
arcing it sharp with a sweep of the whetstone,
waving great circles with a practised air. Old Harry,
who'd always stop to make a boy an aeroplane,
with two bits of kindling, a nail and a story.
Harry, who could slice himself to the bone
and calmly wrap the gash in a paisley handkerchief.
Harry, who knew the time to the nearest half-pint,
and always arrived as my father was drawing
the first foaming glass of a new delivery.

The two of them, old friends, in the sunlit bar,
with the dust motes settling on the faded lino.
My father drawing off the old ale in the pipe,
Harry respectfully waiting for him to finish,
to pour and offer the first glass of the new.

Their ritual was for my father to draw the pint
but never to drink from it. He would hold it aloft
(beers were cloudier in those days), nod sagely
and declare it, *Clear as a bell.* Then he'd sniff
at it and hand it to Harry who would take it,
just as solemnly, sip it and proclaim it… *Passable,*
winking at me as I watched from the door.

I remember the day when Harry came in,
smelling of leather and nettles and grass.
A thin man, old, and wrinkled, and toothless,
full of tales, and the expectation of a pint.
My father nodded, pulled on the beer-engine,
a half-glass, then one he threw away.
Two strong pulls and he held up a pint of mild,
the rich nut-brown ale, glowing like a conker,
the thin foam spilling over his powerful hand.
That's perfect, he said as if to judge and jury.

Harry took the glass but then raised it in salute —
to me who was nine and going away to school.
Here's to you, old'n. Don't forget Old Harry.
Then he put the schooner to his lips and drank it
down in one.
                    He was dead when I came home,
had joined the ranks of those we never spoke about,
for speaking meant remembering and remembering
meant pain. But I held on to his scraps of kindling,
their tang of creosote, and the little nail of love.
and I remembered that morning in the sunlit bar
when old Harry toasted me like a Saxon eoldorman,
his Adam's apple bobbing as he drank my health.
The tilt of his head and the sadness in his eyes.
The passing on of something as old as the beer.

NINETY-SEVEN

He remembered the little black suitcase,
the journeying at peculiar times,
the panic in his mother's eyes,
but he couldn't remember understanding
or having it explained to him
why he was going to Ninety-Seven again
or why his father had become someone else.

He remembered feeling safe at Ninety-Seven,
climbing the stairs to a warm feather bed,
Cornish Wafers and scalded milk,
being tucked-in with a rubber hot-water bottle,
good-night kisses that didn't smell of beer;
but he was still too afraid to ask
how his father could become someone else.

He remembered whisperings at Ninety-Seven,
telephone talk about the coast being clear;
being scrubbed and made presentable,
getting in the back of a big black car.
He remembered the cold as he left Ninety-Seven,
frost on the car and the moonlit road.
He remembered thinking the moon might tell him
why his father had become someone else.

BACK TO THE NUMBERS

You go back to the numbers,
Apollonian numbers,
sky-dry and rarified,
as clean as abstract time.
Back to the numbers,
the mystery of numbers.
Numbers are worth the climb.

When his old Headmaster beat him
in the library at night
while the other boys were sleeping,
when the Hand of Authority slipped and strayed
from neck to back and down between his legs,
he counted things; anything,
volumes of Churchill, T.E. Lawrence
or sometimes the dozens of little punched holes
that covered Authority's polished brogues.

It was back to the numbers,
the safety in numbers,
sky-dry and rarified,
as rare as you can find.
Back to the numbers,
the sanctuary of numbers,
leaving all feeling behind.

LITTLE SOLDIERS

They used to come to her at night, the nine-year-olds,
long after lights out when everything was lonesome.

Maclean had been the first, and later young Bracey,
Bracey who was so much gentler than the others.

He'd knocked so quietly that she hadn't heard him
till his slippers had squeaked on the polished linoleum.

He'd been walking away when she called him back,
head down, hands in his dressing-gown pockets.

Maclean said you might have an aspirin, Matron.
And then through the fog of tiredness. *Can't sleep.*

She took him into her room and sat him on her bed
while the little pill fizzed in its tumbler of water

and then she sat beside him, waited as he drank,
waited till he sagged against her, like a tired pup.

He smelled the same as most young boarders, of piss
and polish and abandonment, yet he seemed different,

so she had cuddled him, like her own, until he sobbed,
and run a tender hand through his corn-coloured hair.

Then like her own, she had gently sent him back to bed
only this time the Head's wife had been lying in wait.

We think it only proper that we keep a certain distance.
And of course, at the end of term, they had to let her go.

Driving her to the station, the Head had been quite direct.
Fact of the matter is we're paid to turn out soldiers.

DEBTOR'S MOON

Two o'clock in the morning and the moon
is fingering the furniture like a bailiff.

The father, in flight from the shame
that nails him to the moment, is lying

unconscious, an outstretched hulk,
a pissed and dissipated Sistine Adam,

nicotine-gilded fingers pointing
towards his empty, brown-bottle god.

The boy has tried to drag him to bed.
He is twelve now. He has failed.

As he sits, benumbed, a foraging mouse
appears in the crook of his father's arm.

The boy calls out but nothing happens.
He is empty, dumb, becoming invisible.

The father mutters, shifts and snores.
The mouse takes fright and vanishes.

The boy stays, watching over his father,
and the moon slips through the trees.

EDDIES AND VORTICES

It had become a house of dull knives,
tattered cuffs and empty bottles.
There were no pictures on the walls
and music had long since fled.
The clock was a run-down contemptuous
Buddha, withdrawn into sullen silence.
In his room, my father was sleeping
it off while, in the kitchen, my mother
was putting the dishes away with just
enough righteous indignation to make
the dogs flinch at every resentful clatter.
The very air was thick with the ghosts
of arguments, unfinished and withheld,
spinning through the angry atmosphere,
creating eddies and vortices, feeding
the house's circular rage.
                                    Somewhere
a draught whistled in the woodwork,
howled and hooted, moaned and died,
as my father began to sing in his sleep.

NEVER

The night my father died
he hit me.
In an extremity of pain

or whisky-rage or both,
one arm dead already,
he lashed out with the other

to send me spinning
across the floor,
more shamed than truly hurt.

I took my tears and hid them,
nursed them
till I heard him on the stairs.

I'm sorry I hit you, he said
and I waited.
Let's make it up, old son.

Never — I spat out years
of resentment.
Never — and I turned away.

He left me then, and later
when I found him
the word was in the air.

Never — the dead forget
but a single word
can ride the living for life.

HIS SUIT

Can't remember much about the funeral
except that I wore my father's suit.
Not his Sunday best, there wasn't one,
but a blue serge striped affair that hung
at odd places on my adolescent body
whilst elsewhere it seemed unnaturally tight.
I'm not sure whose idea it was,
but I wore that suit like a shaman wears
an animal skin, the smell of his tobacco
lingering in the material, the memory
of his final, mad descent enveloping me
like a cloak of tribal secrets.
                                    Back home,
amongst the bridge rolls and the whispers,
my severe Aunt Vera buttonholed me.
She must have spotted the suit because
she held me, gently fingering the lapels.
You're the head of the family now, she said,
and suddenly that old suit stank of beer.
I nodded back at her, just like my father,
smiling weakly as my shoulders sagged.

AROUND AND BELOW AND BEHIND

Across his shoulders anger
and down his knotted spine,
coiled and writhing, captive, bound;
the anger of a thousand yeses
in place of a solitary no.

Moulded round the anger,
corroded, cracked and dangerous,
the armour of his given-shame;
a second hand-me-down inheritance
from those who could not, would not love.

Far below the shame a grief,
unacknowledged, unexpressed;
the oily sea beneath a cliff;
quiescent now but never leaving,
eroding all with a lap and a kiss.

Behind all this a staring child,
alone, abandoned, terrified;
the quintessential orphan,
frozen by the fear of death
and life, and love, and all he knows.

THE BADGER

Today my hands
want to rip and slash,
my jaws to crush
and my teeth to rend.
I have no shred
of forgiveness in me,
no finer feeling,
no liberal felicities.
Today I am one with
the world's dark verities;
with beak and claw,
with talon and tooth.
Today I am hurting,
and I am dangerous.

PROCESSIONAL

I saw a man give way to grief
As the coffin entered in.
Being strangely moved, I stopped
And kindly said to him.

Did you know her long ago?
He, turning, shook his head.
He looked at me from far away,
Then quietly he said,

I grieve here in my father's place.
I openly weep in the crowd.
I shed the tears he could not shed
As death was not allowed.

You do not grieve. You do not weep.
You do not honour the shroud.
How can you ever learn to live
When death is not allowed?

I waited at the churchyard gate.
I thought that he might stay.
I hoped he'd teach me how to grieve
But he'd quietly slipped away.

THE WATER-CAGE

The grief came up unbidden, like water
slowly percolating through the strata
of the past. It found its level and stayed.

It stayed through the iron days of work
and exhaustion, through the brittle days
of disbelief and thoughtless solicitude.

It dripped through the hollow nights
spent clinging artfully to strangers
and leeched the hope out of crawling mornings.

In staying, it was joined by other griefs,
that through the years had washed together,
grief on grief, eroding chasms and ravines

until in time it was a stream of pain, a river
and at last a sea where I was held immobile,
drowning, in a cage that was a second skin.

The grief came up unbidden, like water
slowly percolating through the strata
of the past. It found its own level. It stayed.

A BREAK IN THE LINE

I tried to find him,
tried to put together all the pieces,
make some sense of who he was,
of who my father's father
might have been.

I never knew him,
never saw but one stiff picture of him
in a uniform behind my grandma,
caught between her softness
and his fear.

Twice I asked my uncle,
begged him for the story of his father,
hoping he would help me mend the line
that linked me to the fathers
of the past.

All he gave me was his silence
and the sense of something other, lying
like a wound between the generations,
something raw and tender
like a bruise.

Nothing but an emptiness,
a silence and the shame that set my father
like an animal against the world,
against the line, against himself,
against his son.

HE WRITES A LETTER TO HIS SON

My son, there are things you need to know,
things about your old man and your family
that have been lying in the darkness
unspoken, denied for over thirty years.

My father, your grandfather, wasn't a monster,
just lonely and driven by the ghosts of the past,
but when he was drunk he was another man
and that man could make a childhood a desert.
Sometimes he wanted to fight me, to wrestle.
Fingers locked, he'd force me to my knees,
to prove he was still my unbeatable father,
though the truth was his world was falling apart
and the only one he could beat was his boy.

The darkest times were the sunny afternoons
when he ordered me to strip while he stood there
screaming at me; flaying my fat, adolescent body,
skinning me alive with the rasp of his tongue.
And yes, of course, he had used me earlier,
had drifted from cuddles and little secrets
to the kind of things that make a mockery
of the link between a father and his son.
The maggot on the hook was that even though
he hurt me, he remained my only source
of love - or so it seemed to the wounded kid
who retreated into food and dreamy isolation.

I like to think that it wasn't my dad
who did these things — that it was the whisky,
the brandy, or some dark incubus — but on days
when I'm living without my skin, I remember
his eyes and my flesh begins to creep.

Then the numbness of the moment comes over me
and I know that it was him, my father,
who crossed the line from neediness to using,
and then blamed me for being abused.

I used to fantasise about telling you
the stories my father made up for me,
before the madness and the drink took hold;
and sometimes I dreamt of taking you to visit
the graves of the old folk I ran to in my loneliness.
I imagined telling you their stories,
and my pride as I introduced you to them,
knowing that their loves would not be forgotten.
At other times I knew that the wounds,
though largely healed, had cut too deep;
that I would never hold you in my arms,
nor show you off, nor promise you the world.

More commonly, I was somewhere in between;
travelling in hope of love and kindness
and a woman who could teach me how to trust.
Well, I faced my edge, and I found the woman
and she showed me how to grow my life.
Nowadays, when my father calls to me
from the depths of his particular hell,
I keep on walking, I hold on to my reality.
Which brings me back to this letter,
to you — the son I will never have.

SAVED

My father doesn't haunt me anymore.
The fear has burned off with the mourning
and the loathing has somehow dissipated.
I'm glad I managed to stop forgiving him.
The holy road of the righteous victim
had become a low, deceitful path.
The truth was, I needed to loathe him first,
to gorge myself on delicate hatreds,
eat till I was sated, bloated like a leech.
Only then could I fall away to forgiveness.

Now when I see him, it's sideways on:
a young man of thirty, before I was born,
matinée-idol looks and a crisp cotton shirt,
silk tie, homburg, maybe even spats.
More often than not he's vulnerable,
an orphan, fitfully whistling to the silence.
He's just seen a girl who is strangely familiar,
and he's watching her, hungering with his eyes.
Now he's a comet, falling towards her —
thinking she is beautiful, thinking he is saved.

CUT GRASS AND NICOTINE

I could tell you about the pity and the waste,
the way I watched him disintegrating,
slowly becoming the bloated wreck
that lay on the floor in a drunken puddle.
Or I could talk about the shame —
that's dangerous because I get stuck again
in the acid limbo that held me back then.
I could tell you about the shock of finding him,
snarling in death and grinning obscenely;
of magically thinking that I had murdered him,
killed my own father with my ill will;
of carrying his corpse for twenty years; falling
to my knees with the weight of his memory.
But it's harder, much harder, even now
to talk about the ache for the spaces where
the quiet atonements might have been made;
to say
        to say
                to say that I still love him,
and that somewhere inside me there's a boy
who pines for the warm and comforting
odour of him, the starched-cotton crispness
softened with sweat and brilliantine,
the cut-grass freshness and the stale cigarettes;
to say after years of bile and bitterness
that sometimes I miss and yearn for my father.

OLD DOGS

Sunday was my father's birthday.
It came and went without my remembering
which is no bad thing considering the extremes
of love and hate that I have felt for him.
Had he lived he would have been a hundred,
a venerable old gentleman, frail and white.
Maybe he could have outlived his ruin,
have transcended the shambles that was his life.
Then again he might simply have wallowed,
waited like a baby in his puddle of Scotch,
hoping for a mother to come to his rescue,
or a wife, or a son, or the Seventh Cavalry.
My guess is that old dogs can't be bothered
and that old drunks rarely redeem themselves.
Still, it's good to think of him at his centenary,
ennobled by the journey, finally arrived,
clean and sober with his dignity recovered.
He may have been dead for half a lifetime
but the son he slumped against still has hope.

III

VOICES IN THE DARK

SURVIVORS

He found a veiled woman
who had seen too much
then tortured her further
by asking her — Why?

She looked at him sadly
through stricken eyes
that seemed to say — Have
you no pain of your own?

Roaring waters filled him.
She blessed his arid eyes.
Better sad than blind — but
better blind than screaming.

DANSE MACABRE

For P. T.

You see something behind their eyes,
a look that says I'd like to hurt you,
a message in the body as it reaches forward,
straining towards you like a dog on a leash;
mouth made cruel, muscles corded,
a flare of the nostrils, an involuntary snarl,
the malevolent flicker of a pink, wet tongue.

In an instant you are shutting down
as if nature itself were compressing you.
Your muscles go limp and volition fails.
The whole world seems to move in treacle.

On the outside no one notices a thing —
people who know you see nothing wrong —
while inside, past and present merge,
conjoining in a dance of ancient finality.
At this point a breath could make a signal
as broad as the gestures of a wild flamenco;
the slightest move confirms your submission
as clearly as if you had offered your neck.

So you freeze, like a fallow deer in the forest,
one hoof raised, in total attention, waiting
for the crash of the clumsy hunter, waiting
for the coming of the shadow of death.
And in your head an old tune circulates —
a nursery rhyme, or the ghost of a song.
The words are lost in a roaring silence
but the message is simple: endure, endure.

TAKE HER DOWN

Maria has been shamed so many times
she apologises with her every move.
Something in her cringes as she listens
to the jangled voices, the inner jury,
rigged always to find her wanting.
She lives in the tentative hope of love
and the luscious fear of what love might bring
but when she faces the bedroom mirror
she can see that love's an exclusive gift
exchanged by the beautiful, not the ugly;
not the fat, the stupid, the disgusting,
the obscene, the dull and the unlovable.

And now she's naked, in his room again,
in his terrible, smiling, sunlit room;
watching his shadow on the dove-grey carpet
as he moves towards her, snarling again.
His words, once tender, now spill like vitriol
over her breasts and her podgy white belly,
eating their way down to burn out her sex;
empty and wasted at thirteen years old...

You make me want to vomit. You're a whore.

She wraps herself in a grease-stained kimono,
sparing the mirror too long a sight of her,
and tiptoes down to the kitchen once more
where she soothes herself with midnight ice-cream,
licking her wounds on the back of a spoon.

CHIRON'S AUBADE

In the end nothing really heals.
The wound remains a hideous wound.
We may lay claim to powers,
knowledge, method and skill,
but all we have is a yen for wellbeing,
a modicum of hope and a desperate need
to make good, to fix, to rearrange the evidence.
What we do is pick at the scab,
peel it away for the sake of knowing,
worry and tug until tissue comes too,
opening the flesh to the old invasions.
Let us not pretend to healing —
better admit to our own desire
for meaning and control in an arbitrary world
that knows neither peace nor restitution.
They order things better in the forest —
revenge then learning, blood then understanding:
no chatter, no white coats, no pointless erudition,
just retribution and a cold dry wisdom
bleeding into the truth of the world.

FLASHBACK

It's like this. Something kicks it off —
a sharp word, a noise, the soughing of the wind,
an unexpected, complex animal smell —
a thing that is not exactly of the event
but close enough to make the leap,
to confound the present and loop back to the past,
to make of a breeze, or the lemon scent of polish,
a trigger that re-enacts the moment.
Not a drama, with its little lies and embellishments,
its opportunities for creating a bit of mileage,
but the real thing, complete and inescapable,
total immersion in the event itself;
exactly as it happened, in every fibre of your body:
the skin becoming clammy, the chill, the rigidity,
the shutting down of your stomach and liver,
the bile in your throat that is really adrenaline,
the bitter taste that comes with survival.
What you see without seeing, what you hear
without hearing, are the crystals
of memory dissolving in your blood.
Suddenly you are acting from another, older place,
living in two times simultaneously:
your mind alerted, with its calculating edge,
your subtle heart banished to unreachable safety;
the old reptile part of you hanging on,
ready to do anything to get back to the dark,
to peace, to the cool embrace of silence;
and if that means lashing out or hurting, if that
means wounding with tooth, or tongue, or blade,
so be it.

Afterwards the shame, the shaky hands, the staring,
the reinventions of history, the never-ever-agains.
I have hurt the people that I have loved most dearly,
and try as I may, the truth is, I could hurt them again.
My hope, as the spiral winds down to its centre,
is that they might come to look at me
without an edge of fear.

THE MEDICAL ROOM

*On learning that D.H. his old teacher
had been tried and convicted*

He remembered being marked out as a liar,
being made to stand on an Ercol chair
adrift on a sea of polished parquet
while the rest of the school ate prunes around him.

He remembered the letter which informed his parents
that he was no more than a rotten apple
in danger of contaminating the rest of the barrel —
no mean feat for an eleven-year-old.

And he certainly remembered the ritual after games,
the shivering queue of naked schoolboys
running the gauntlet of six hot showers,
each boy halted under the cold;
made to pirouette three times in front of him,
juddering and jumping, as he stood there,
naked too — *making sure no one caught a cold.*

But he couldn't remember a single teacher
Saying, *Something's wrong*, or stepping in to stop it,
though they must have noticed the breakdowns
and the truancy, the gradual diminishment,
the shrinking of the boys who waited after school,
shame-faced, silent, outside the Medical Room.

And that was the thing, the cruel thing,
the one dark thing he could never remember.

Not after years of counselling and therapy,
of 12-step meetings and self-help seminars,
circles and processes, group work and anger work,
of coming to terms with the rage and the childlessness;
learning that victims need not turn into perpetrators,
discovering that he wasn't rotten to the core,
discovering that sometimes the gift is to forget.

Even after finding and accepting love,
of allowing himself to be held by another;
even when he learned about the trial and conviction,
that some last part of him was finally safe;
even then, though he tried, he could never remember
what happened in the Medical Room.

IV

WALKING DOWN
INTO THE WATER

MAN TO MAN

I shall spare you my pain
because I am English,
because I am understated,
because I am my father's son
and because the tipsy ghosts
of our forefathers
are floating in the air about us
like a regiment of butlers,
swaying slightly to and fro,
eyeing me suspiciously.

I can spare you my pain
because I am strong,
because I am practised,
because I'm a right-hard bastard
and because the dogs I've kicked
like the women I've fucked
know that I'm well-tasty,
that I like a drink on Fridays,
and if they want goodies
that's part of the deal.

I will spare you my pain
because I am numb,
because I am vulnerable,
because I'm up against the wall
and because the wall holds back
the boundless waters of my grief.
If it gave we'd all be swept away
but I daren't tell you that
because you're a man
and nobody trusts a man — ever.

GATHERING AT THE GATE

Deep suspicion darkly rounded
Bodies nursing fears well founded
Hungry ghosts by fathers hounded
To our meeting by the gate

Some in awe of rage unspoken
Most in boyhood nearly broken
All prepared to pay the token
Pay in passing through the gate

Work-bound men achievement driven
Long lost boys their shames unshriven
Men who ache to be forgiven
At our meeting by the gate

Without prompting without urging
Comes a story comes a purging
One by one their truths emerging
From the shadows by the gate

Somewhere in those shadows prowling
Near to pain and close to howling
Something stirring something growling
In the darkness by the gate

Maleness stronger for its weeping
Kept the man-child safely sleeping
There's a sense that we'll be keeping
To our meeting by the gate
In the shadows by the gate
In the darkness by the gate

COMFORT

For P. A.

A solid man, he's seen a thing or two,
enough to be assured of his place in the world.
The lines that are deepening into creases,
the greying stubble and the clear, kindly gaze,
speak of the journey from naivety to despair
and on to a hard-won, tempered acceptance.
Tonight though, his eyes are moist with memories
evoked by the awkward, tentative sound
of his friends in the kitchen singing hymns.
There are fragments, verses, starts and beginnings,
followed by the swoop of remembered choruses —
the rumbling summons of a half-forgotten past.

Gripped by more than musical nostalgia,
he's caught on the point of a genuine grief.
Images surface to discomfit and unsettle him,
the washed-out snaps of a sepia time.

As a lad I never thought Suffolk was flat.
The elms were like hills around the village,
and the towers of the churches split the sky:
Southwold, Blythburgh, Walberwick.
They were my Alps, my Himalayas....

A rousing chorus floats in from the kitchen,
carrying a remembrance of harvest homes.
There are tears now, welling and tumbling,
and the threat of a deep irrepressible sob.
He doesn't fight it, he lets it come
and with it the memory of consolations
that made rural poverty bearable:

the rooky fields, the stark November trees,
and the sonorous calling of the village bells:
Sundays and holidays, Christmas and Easter,
the careful monotony of the passing bell,
and once in a blue moon, now and again,
the rolling glory that was ringing the changes:
over the fields, through the wide Suffolk sky,
the comforting call of a long-forgotten god.

THE LADS IN THE PARK

Why do the young lads bellow in the park
and spoil the calm of a long summer's evening?

Perhaps they've forgotten something.
Perhaps they want salt but not vinegar.
Perhaps their little-boy voices just broke
and they think they need some man-practice.

Maybe they're in the movies.
Maybe they're on a mission.
Maybe there's suddenly a girl across the way
with a smile that only responds to bellowing.

Perhaps they're feeling isolated.
Perhaps they're feeling inadequate.
Perhaps they're feeling abandoned — though
the odds are they're not feeling anything at all.

Maybe if they didn't bellow they'd explode.
Maybe they're going to explode anyway.
Maybe the stillness scares them so much
they need the simple reassurance of an explosion.

Perhaps they're waiting to be told to shut up.
Perhaps they've been told to shut up already.
Perhaps they're sick of being called boys
long after their forefathers would have been men.

Then again they might just bellow 'cos they're lads,
'cos that's what lads have to do to get noticed,
and 'cos this sad and middle-aged world of ours
needs shaking, every generation, with a shout.

SMALL PARTING

Larry, the flatmate, left today.
We'd shared the place for a year or two;
argued over rent, laughed sometimes
and, on one occasion, grieved together
when his cat was killed by a careless driver.
Nothing remarkable about this small parting
except he couldn't bring himself to say goodbye
and I couldn't be fussed to cross the hall
as he slammed and banged and swore at boxes,
letting us know he was leaving in mid-dudgeon.
Odd how he needed to be angry to leave.
I used to quit jobs that way, one after the other,
using petty quarrels to break my attachments
like an eaglet, squabbling its way from the eyrie,
when all it has to do is fly.
                              Anyway, he left,
while I sat at the kitchen table and waited,
thinking to wave when he passed outside.
I heard him swearing his way along the hallway
and the crustle of his last black plastic bag.
There was a pause before the door shut, finally,
and he clumped his way past the kitchen window.
I raised my hand with a certain practiced irony
but he was deliberately looking away –
eyes down, jaw set, unable even to look at me.
Thus we parted, me feeling graceless, shabby
and cheap, and him with all his baggage.

DARSHAN

For 'Carlos' who didn't make it

A lattice of scar tissue covers his face,
and the eyes are hooded by swollen brows.
What you see is what you get: a wreck,
a boxer who's taken too many blows,
a man who's come in like a wandering pi-dog,
anxious yet hungry, desperate to settle.

Fuck it, I'm tired, fellas. I'm really tired.

He wants to do good, he says, to serve;
like the time in Calcutta when he was a kid.
He was just a junkie with nowhere to go
but the Sisters of Charity gave him a job
and a few rupees to keep him going.
All he had to do was bring in the dying.

I was using their money to buy my dope.

His head goes down and suddenly he's sobbing.
The story comes out in a series of grunts.
One time Mother Theresa was in the passageway.
He was pushed towards her by Sister Audrey.

Mother, this is Carl. He wants to see you.

Carlos froze as the tiny avatar cocked her head,
looked at him from beneath her blue-lined sari

He's fifty now and will never get sober,
but that was a moment that saw him through:
the blessing from the wrinkled little woman,
the eyes that saw, and loved, and forgave.

I'm a piece of shit – you know that, fellas –
but while she was looking at me, I was clean.

TEARS ON THE DRUM

For R.B.

We are standing together, my long-lost brother and I,
On the sloping deck of a holed and dying luxury liner.
We are sharing a fine cigar because we have no jokes.
He is talking about the grandfathers who went before.

Today I understand how these proud men,
Lonely and afraid, could rise up smiling
In far-off, strange, unhallowed places
With mud on their tongues and tears on the drum;

How they could gather, to pick sweet poppies,
The red, red poppies, and when they were gathered,
To walk together, into the morning,
The misty morning, and die together.

We need to weep awhile, my long-lost brother and I
But we both know the score — there's never the time.
So we wave once more at the distant boats. Then
We smile, hold hands, and walk down into the water.

MAKING FOR BENARES

We sat awhile and contemplated the departing river
And, as we flowed together in companionable silence,
We saw our fathers' giant lives becoming smaller,
No more than the wrack of their driftwood dreams.

It wasn't the abuse that broke us but the absence,
The ragged, gaping hole that's felt by bitter sons in exile.
We would have been warriors but there was no land.
We could have been lovers but we knew no love.

Instead, we burned like pyres in the angry copper light,
Our hearts too full to open to the whispers of the past.
Let us now consign our rusted armour to the river.
We tried. We failed. We learned to weep;
                              We deserve this tender peace.

SOMETHING WE DON'T TALK ABOUT

The beauty of men lies in the doing:
in a love that notices when things need fixing;
that mows the lawn, that feeds the dog,
that crosses vast oceans to bring home a nutmeg.

The beauty of men lies in the dancing:
in the wildness of youth, in the cackle of age,
in the furious stamp and the delicate gesture
that flies like a hawk from the wrist of a huntress.

The beauty of men lies in the silence:
the silence that speaks of the bloody fields;
of the distant wave, the encouraging smile,
and the song that was lost on the long road home.

MAMMA'S BOY

Wanting to say something to his mother;
wanting to say no, or, more exactly,
not now, not here, not in this room
with all these familiar people watching,

Wanting to say something to his mother
about love and control and the gift
of manhood – which isn't really hers to give
but his to claim, or steal, or simply demand
by holding up a firm, implacable hand.

Wanting all this but managing no more
than another rueful, apologetic smile;
the dip of the head and the yielding silence
which killers know as a rage deferred.

STANDING IS A GIFT

He comes at me because he must.
Sitting there, fat and in my fifties,
I am everything he loathes, and fears.
In his sight, I'm all the bosses,
teachers, badges, caps and uniforms,
all the bullies he's had to defer to.
I am the enemy. I am dad.

He snaps a sidelong scowl at me,
burning eyes under hooded lids,
but in that fire, if you cared to look,
you might catch the glint of something
slithering, ancient and implacable,
towards this thing he needs to kill.

It doesn't land straight, of course,
not in these sideways, sophisticated days;
it arrives as a sly yet casual aside;
a petty, sneering, yet practiced swipe
that shows a clear intellectual grasp
but has the slick of bile about it,
the sticky slick of a young man's hate.

I'm struck by a blast of desiccating heat
that emanates from the rage inside this boy
though what comes to mind is a desert street
where a tired sheriff is being stalked
by a kid who wants to shoot him in the back
because it's the Wild West and he knows
there's only one way to become a gunslinger.

So we sit there, sizing each other up
me with my worn and battered badge,
him with a look between murder and tears,
I want to say, *Does it have to be this way?*
but I know that it does – at least for him.

And that decides me. Standing is my gift.
I cross to the swing-doors of the saloon
which clatter as I step out into the sunshine.
I pause a moment to be sure of his footfall
then leave the sidewalk for the dusty street.

FAMOUS LAST WORDS

Someone once explained to me, patiently,
as if to an idiot, that Horatio Nelson
had never said *Kiss me Hardy*,
he merely said, *Kismet*, meaning fate,
meaning that's how the ship's biscuit crumbles.
But I've been spending time this summer
listening to men, and observing them;
watching how their worried shoulders speak,
their capable hands, their constant tension,
their silences, their yearning for affection.
I've been thinking of that tiny admiral's uniform,
the one with the Nile Star and the bullet hole,
and I have a sense of Nelson dying, shot
through the back in his moment of triumph;
Nelson, after years of hardtack and seasickness,
of discipline, and 'the exigencies of the service'.
Nelson, self-sacrificed piecemeal over the years,
dying on the altar of a nation's yearning.
And I have a sense of a great door opening
in a heart long starved of tenderness;
I see him looking at the faces in the Cockpit,
waiting for his friends and followers to join him,
and I see his eyes, through the telescope of pain,
holding on to Hardy as they waited for the ebb.
I see the feeling that a man can hold for another
when they've worked together for half a lifetime.
It was love that spoke – and not to history.
Of course he said it: *Kiss me, Hardy*

V

DWINDLING
IN THE DUSK

A CERTAIN CLOSENESS

He picks up the phone and calls his mother.
It's been a while. They're not that close.

The tremble in her voice reminds him she's afraid.
A generation is dying around her, falling away
in ones and twos: today a friend, yesterday a brother-in-law,
tomorrow the woman across the way she always smiled at
but never got close to.

They talk around things – jobs and bosses, aches and pains –
but the silences speak of resentment and regret,
of the lost opportunities that made them who they are,
of passing trains that sped through the night.
How could they even begin to get close?

This grey-haired old darling, popular and well-beloved,
was once the terror of his childhood:
brittle, unpredictable, scared into lovelessness.
This was the mother of the shrivelled heart
who mocked him in public and shamed him in private,
the goddess who cursed him, who walked away.
And now she wants to get close.

On the telephone she says, *I love you* – words
he chased for thirty years; and when he visits, once a month,
she seems reluctant to let him go. Then, when he leaves
to catch his train, she follows him out into the night
whispering, *Love you*, to his retreating back.

So sometimes, when the day leaves him chopped inside,
he thinks of calling her and saying how he feels,
though that would risk a certain closeness.

Instead he sits by his window and thinks of her,
waiting in the stillness as the evening falls.
The two tied together, separated by continents,
scant miles apart, and dwindling in the dusk.

HER MANTRA

I'm so worried. I'm so worried. I'm so worried.
What's wrong, Mother?
I'm so worried. I'm so worried. I'm so worried.
What's the matter?
I'm so worried. I'm so worried. I'm so worried.
What is it?
I haven't got any clothes.

Alright, we'll find you some, says my wife.
Any excuse to get out of the nursing home.
Marks and Sparks suit you? John Lewis?
Come on then. Let's take you out for the day.

Her tiny frame beetling down racks of pastels,
grim mouth practising disappointment.
Right size, wrong colour. Right colour, wrong size.
And then the shock of something scarlet —
screaming, no-better-than-she-ought-to-be red.
A thick, heavy cardigan with military buttons.
A guilty little smile gives her pleasure away
as smell and touch now do their work
and her birdlike hand drifts over the material.
Soon there's a basket of silky white blouses,
slips and things she insists on calling 'smalls'.

At the checkout she beams like a visiting duchess,
tells an assistant that her hair looks pretty.
In the car she hums a long-forgotten tune.
Then, back in her room, she sinks onto the bed….

I'm so worried. I'm so worried. I'm so worried.
What is it now, Mother?
I'm so worried. I'm so worried. I'm so worried.
What's wrong?
I'm so worried. I'm so worried. I'm so worried.
But we got you clothes!
I've got nowhere to put them.

A LITTLE YES

My mother doesn't really know me.
A look comes over her, as she bolts her food
or gulps her scalding, nursing-home tea,
that says, who's this dodgy-looking man
with his stuck-up voice and work-shy hands?

I should be hurt by this, but I'm not.
Firstly, she never had much of a handle on me,
was always too self-absorbed to listen
to my desperate attempts to impress or inform.
And secondly, she's tiny now, diminished,
less than half the woman who used to scare me
by telling me she was going to kill herself,
or throw herself downstairs, or run away;
who at twelve I once found in the bathroom,
pissed and staring at a razorblade,
unable to live but unwilling to do the deed.

Before she was diagnosed, we'd got to the stage
where we practised the love
that we thought we should feel, but even then
she would occasionally whack me
with a royally casual, *What is it you do, dear?*

Today I am sitting with her, on her bed,
in the beige little room that is now her world.
She is quiet, and trembling, like a little girl,
a bundle of old shames, fears and loneliness.

I try to make conversation. It doesn't work.
We lapse into emptiness more than silence.
Do you want a cuddle? I say at last.
She nods a little, *Yes,* and sags against me.
There is nothing of her. She's almost gone.
I put my arm around her — still trying hard.

THE GRANDMOTHERS

The Grandmothers hover in the spaces
where long-dismantled walls once met;
in bricked-up casements and lost galleries;
resigned, abiding, waiting to be asked.

Beneath this old lintel, two sisters
lean against each other, gently
swaying backwards and forwards,
their feelings bleeding into the masonry.

That threshold over there still resonates
to childbed fears, to moans and cries.
A midwife leaves, a coffin arrives,
a family's sobs and sighs remain.

And when at last a building crumbles,
falling away like flesh from the bone,
these presences are left, imprinted,
hanging like cobwebs in the trembling air.

These are the places where, in our hurry,
We leave little pieces of our souls behind.
Some part of me then has departed already.
The Grandmothers welcome me, hovering, kind.

A VISIT

This evening, for a while,
as I sat in the gathering darkness, alone,
my mother, who died some years ago,
came to me – or rather surfaced within me –
so that my pursed lips became her pursed lips,
her fidgety hands my fidgety hands,
her wary eyes my wary eyes.
                              We sat together
no more than a moment, my mother and I,
and then, in the flutter of an eyelid,
she gently moved on – though for that second,
while I sat in her tired, anxious skin,
I understood, and forgave, and was terrified.

VI

MEETING THE GODDESS

MY LITTLE MAN

What's all the shouting about?
asks one of two thin Islington women,
indicating the hall next door.

Some kind of uniformed organisation,
says the other, darkly,
squinting through the narrow glass.

Nazis…? No, Wolf Cubs, says the elder.
Little Nazis. Quite harmless actually.
Only six or seven years old.

All be over soon then, says the first.
They'll all be turning into eight-year-olds.
Ghastly! they say together.

Just then, as if to prove the point,
in a burst of boisterous caps and badges,
the pack comes tumbling through:

a dozen energised, excited boys,
each full of life and yelling his part in it,
till, just as quickly, they're off and away.

The women shudder involuntarily,
repelled, as if they've seen a crime.
They hold a battered, trampled silence.

I know a boy, says the elder at last.
You'd never catch him behaving like that.
But then he's from a very good family.

And as she speaks she conjures up
a pale and thoughtful eight-year-old,
standing alone at the foot of her bed.

She reaches out a hand and strokes him,
feeling his resistance fade.
Perfect, she whispers. *My little man.*

FROZEN RABBIT

Was it Sue? Forgive me, I've forgotten her name
though I've never forgotten the taste of her mouth
or the tantalising smell of her cheap perfume.
Yes, and the unbelievable fullness of her
when she gave me the keys to her young body.
Me, the fat and spotty fourteen-year-old
who could barely imagine what sex might be like.

The party, I remember, was decorous and tidy,
on a tidy estate in a tidy little town.
The music was the Beatles, and I was a rebel,
waiting for love and a whiff of Sgt Pepper.

Somehow we'd got into the dangerous dark
that beckoned around the side of the house. She let me
kiss her, kissed me back, till, like a record-player,
we went automatic and I became a Rolling Stone.
My hands, the same clumsy adolescent hands
that had failed the tests of button and bra-strap,
were suddenly as accomplished as a violinist,
as safe as Gordon Banks. I cupped her breasts,
like Bobby Moore holding two World Cups,
and for the first time I sensed a woman opening
to me — ardent, willing and unashamed.

I also remember that this was the moment
when the headlights caught us, pinning us to the wall,
and that my hands became fused to her breasts,
immovable, frozen, rigid with astonishment
as I recognised her father coming to take her
home.

ACROSS A CROWDED ROOM

Who's that? What an extraordinary face.
And look at those eyes, amazing eyes.
Kind of — familiar. She's looking over here.
You could get lost in those eyes.

I wonder if we've met before?
It's as if we know each other already.
Maybe we were lovers in another life,
long ago, like Antony and Cleopatra.

Yes, we're probably an ongoing item.
We came together: we were torn apart.
We loved, we lost, we betrayed each other,
compelled by an all-consuming passion.

And now we've spotted each other again.
Venus and Mars will collide right here.
There'll be sparks, desire, a couple of children,
separations and tearful reconciliations.

Finally one of us is going to call it a day.
They're going to croak and desert the other one.
I don't know why we bother, really.
Here she comes... *What are you looking at?*

NIGHT MUSIC

Tonight the stars are broken glass.
He has no one to touch but himself.

He could go back to the midnight shop,
cruise the high metallic racks,
buy himself a pliant lover,
take her home and slowly undress her,
page by glossy page

but the stars would still be broken glass.
There'd be no one to touch but himself.

Later, he might cross the river,
take his ever-growing compulsion
to meet the girls that businessmen meet
under the arches of excitement
where money and numbers no longer do it

but the stars would still be broken glass.
After the business he'd be alone.

He could call her, right now, call her
and say that he wanted to hold her,
meaning he wanted her to hold him
but they both know that he'd be lying.
They never held. He cut straight to sex.

Tonight the stars are broken glass.
He has no one to hold but himself.

BOWERBIRDS

Basically it's their youth he hates,
even more than their beauty;

the lustrous, not-quite-ripeness
of them, the endless possibilities.

Everyone's in love this evening,
and worse, they're only twenty-one.

Couples dotted along the river,
staking out their mating territories;

turning bench after public bench
into deeply private arbours

where, like bowerbirds,
they mime the wordless rituals

of gift and tentative gift; of blush
and glance and touch and kiss.

Alone now, he has come to loathe
their easy, unforced intimacies;

the gazing and the stroking,
and the play of lips on grateful skin.

Their hungry kisses make him shrink
as his skin crawls to the kiss of envy

and every elegant, youthful gesture
makes him older, sadder, emptier.

THE SAME OLD SONG

Fuck, fuck, fuck!
I've done it now.
Said far too much.
Said all the things
I promised
I'd never, ever say again.

Fuck! I can't believe it.
I've given it all away.
Muttered those little truths
That leave you
Feeling like offal
Slithering down a pipe.

Fuck! I've really blown it.
I've made declarations,
Unreasonable demands.
Oh fuck — I've even made a deal.
Thing is, I'm all confused:
Am I in love again,
Or is this just bronchitis?

IN FROM THE DARK

Barely house-broken, he comes to her
downcast but alert, offering her a stone,
a leaf, a feather that he hopes might show
the wonder that he feels and needs to share.
Every tiny gift, each incremental gesture,
brings the timber wolf closer to the fire.
Now trembling, now curious, now aching
for affection, he stalks the warmth and light.
Sidling in from the forest of experience,
mind alive to the first false move, tense
body listening for the dry snap of memory,
he circles slowly round the flames, shudders,
then lays his head upon her lap.
                                        This is how
the wildness dies. This is how we come in.

A TRUCE TOO SOON

I have no answer to the anger of women,
the resentment I see in a small, balled fist,
in a wire-taut smile, in a trembling chin.

I have no response to the hatred I see
that defers and defers and defers to the male
yet revenges itself upon innocent boys.

I have no reply to the old, cold loathing
that slithers behind my lover's eyes,
keeping me watchful and wakeful beside her.

No, I've no answer to the anger of women,
no answer beyond a slow understanding,
a terror, and the age-old rage of men.

SPENT

A thick August night
with the slow air stunned
and the world come down
to a melting maze
of arms and legs
and heads on thighs;
to the rising and falling
of bellies and nipples,
and to one hand moving,
exhausted but demanding,
running beads of sweat
together as it slides,
beyond all relief,
from pleasure to pleasure,
to pleasure, to pleasure....

AS EASY AS FALLING

Love me she said, opening to him like a well

but
love me
became
save me
and
save me
became
use me
and
use me
became
hurt me,
like they
hurt me
before.
So
he did,
he
hurt her
and
it was
all
so easy,
as easy
as using,
as easy
as losing,
as easy
as
falling
down
a well-
used
well.

THE DECENT THING

It was her body, of course, her call, her choice.
What their awkwardness had made together
was a burden, an encumbrance to her. Palely
he had offered marriage, had felt the chains
of responsibility leap as the hull of his life
had careered down the slipway; gone before
even the band arrived.
                              I don't want it, she said
and he had winced... *You'd better get it fixed...*
So he had done the decent thing, had found
the money she despised, had borrowed
and worked the extra hours; then gone with her
to the seaside town where he had stood, alone
and ashamed, as the bright assistants had fussed
around her, and the busy consultant had done
the business, had made all safe, and clean,
                              and forgettable.
Outside, on the beach, as he waited in the rain,
he heard the words he would never speak,
would never throw at her, even in temper, even
on the day that she walked away. Some poor
idiot was shouting at the shingle, his flat
voice skimming over the rain-stunned water.
It was my kid too, you know. It was my kid too.

STAG

Oooh Lovely!

What is it about the very word 'marriage'
that has rational people squealing like pigs?
What part of this trite, commercial transaction
sets their eyes agleam, like a fire sale or a car crash?
Is it the prospect of another empty ceremony,
the dull flat drone of the inauthentic minister,
the meaningless farrago of thees and thous?
Or is it the parading of trophy and conquest,
the public triumph of ownership:
the suppression of the singular,
the death of the wild, the extinction
in another of their own surrendered flame?

Aaah Bless!

SALT WOMAN *

Salt Woman, hidden in a world of tears,
I heard you sobbing but I would not comfort you;
Hearing not a lover but the mother of sores,
Banished and shunned in a hundred tellings.

I had forgotten you. I had abandoned you
Yet still you came to me in birdsong and dreaming.
And I was afraid of you, afraid of your giving —
your wild embrace, impassioned as the wind.

Heart Woman, vanished to a lake of salt,
I heard you calling but I could not answer you.
And now that I see you, now that I can honour you,
Everything has savour, but you are gone.

* The Story of Salt Woman – from the Pueblo peoples of the South Western United States – speaks of a fabled woman made of salt who was shunned by the people until they belatedly realised that her crystal fingers could give their food savour – by which time she had vanished into the Great Salt Lake. Since then it has been the task of men to pan for salt in the distant lake – and to do so by panning backwards whilst weeping – a sacred atonement to the divine feminine.

A WORD

(For B & L on the occasion of their marriage)

It's sad to think we might have lost
Those rich and rumbling Jacobean cadences
Which stirred and comforted our ancestors
In times of woe and joy and need,
Those weighted, freighted, archaic words
That uplifted, admonished and held the soul.

Blessed art thou...
Let not your heart be troubled...
Faith, hope, charity, these three —
But the greatest of these is charity....

I've heard that the Inuit of Alaska
Have a hundred ways of describing snow,
That the Ifaluk on their atoll in the South Pacific
Have innumerable words for kinds of anger —
Lingeringer, nguch, tipmochmoch, song.
Once we had charity, now we just have love,
And love is an overburdened word.

Let us then wish our dear friends charity,
A broadening and a deepening, a growing care,
A kinder, wiser, more courageous caritas
That meets the world and all that it can do;
A love that can soothe an ailing toddler,
Yet still burn bright at the end of the day;
A love that travels, out there and back again,
A love that can wait, in patience, and awe;
A love that accepts, a love that allows,
A love that can trust when it doesn't understand;

A living companionship, a learnt compassion,
A quiet meeting of hands, and hearts, and minds.

So, let us now vouchsafe them both this quality,
Which *vaunteth not itself* and *is not puffed up*.
May they cleave together many years in charity.
May they come to know more than just plain love.

CONISTON WATER

Going down
for the first time,
all he could hear
was the water in his ears
and the squeal of a toddler
somewhere on the shore.
The second time,
he heard the rush
of a lifetime,
polishing the stones
of his inadequacies.
But the third time,
the last time,
he felt the sound
and it ripped at him,
tore him like a tooth.
What filled his ears
when he finally went
under was the rending
ripple of her laughter.

HE TAKES A LITTLE POP
AT THE MOTHER-IN-LAW

Families again — hers this time, not his.
What you don't want, you get. What you need,
they can never give you.
                          Her mother takes
a small, slightly nondescript molehill
and turns it into a veritable alp: a loose word
here, some family politics there, a couple
of assumptions and a downright lie.
Within hours the whole demented pack
of us are seething, twisted, ready to pop
while she, the architect of countless dramas,
sits feigning innocence and baffled incomprehension.
There's a certain kind of selfish old woman
who cannot relinquish the power of motherhood,
whose latter years are a rearguard action,
a resentful retreat in the face of youth.
Defeat follows defeat and slowly, inevitably,
the things that could have been gracefully surrendered
are snatched away by exasperated children.
There are victories, of course, nasty little routs,
triumphs to be carried to the grave and beyond.
Her daughter is left with the corrosive certainty
that she will always be less than mummy,
while her son, her darling, the apple of her eye,
stays emasculated, tied to the stake of her charm.
The loathing she felt for her children's father
drips like vitriol into their lives, drama by drama,
commotion by commotion, slowly weakening them,
making them smaller – stifling, silencing, murdering.

IT TURNS AND SOFTLY SPEAKS

Night after night the empty road,
the home-light diminishing then vanishing
as you travel out into the world again,
hungry for a love that you can never allow.

If only you could pause for a moment,
look down at your feet and not at the horizon,
you might spot the small grey pebble of love
lying discarded where you flung it as a child.

What was the hurt that made you a loner?
How did the wondrous gift become a wound?
You're alone. You're still giving
but you're giving from an exhausted place.
Listen to the call of love: admit, accept, receive.

VII

IN THE SECRETIVE NIGHT

CHASING THE FISHERMAN

Here it comes — another workshop poem,
quietly descriptive, and nicely judged;
a low-key, continent, and well-wrought lyric
imbued with an element of difficulty:
not quite obscure but acceptably mysterious;
furnished and burnished with liberal angst.

Oh bollocks! – I want to write a poem
filled with a rage of ancestral bones;
a poem of old chants, challenges and hakas,
a howl, a snarl, an indictment, a charm,
a mantra with anger flying like spittle,
a piece with a blood-price, with dirt on its hands;

that poem from Porlock, from Reading, from Chile,
that poem from Belsen, from over the wire;
a poem by Crow out of Anna Akhmatova,
a poem that gets me to the passionate dawn.

HAMLET IN HAIKU

Hamlet in haiku
A few syllabiloquies
And the kid snuffs it

THREE HAIKU

i

Pheasants on a branch
The last rooks trailing homeward
Rosehips in the mud

ii

Finches quarrelling
A painted hedgerow plundered
God, I hate haiku!

WE KNOW WHAT WE LIKE

We're going to see
that blockbuster movie:
the one based on
the smash hit musical,
which came from
the big television series,
inspired by the show,
whose book derived
from the documentary
about the film,
of the play, of the opera,
adapted from the novel
which came from
that brilliant radio play;
or was it the best-selling
audio book, adapted
from the biography
that won that award,
about the guy on television.
You know, whatshisname.
We love anything original.

PERFECT

Like this, like a revelation, here and now,
a moment that a lifetime's work has led to.
Here, in the kitchen, in the middle of the night
with Juliet asleep and the moonlit world made
transitory.
                    A stirring, an idea, a latent image,
something waiting to be fashioned, to be born.
But then, when it manifests, to simply let it go:
no making, no object; no lens to catch or capture it;
neither canvas, nor paper, nor limiting stone.
Just a moment of itself, like a sunset or a kiss:
like the time Mark Rylance stepped aside
to let Shakespeare himself appear before us;
or the night Nigel North with his delicate lute
became the very strength and comfort of Bach.
Yes, to surrender, to embrace the ephemeral,
to allow what is perfect to vanish away.
Maybe now, sitting here in the secretive night
with the old house settling, grumbling around me.
A man, alone, with the pieces of his life,
the immensity of death, and the sweetness
                                        of everything.

DEAD POET

It's good to be dead, to have the leisure
to talk to someone who might want to listen;
to be a poet at last, I mean a real poet, dead
as a doornail and so somehow more believable.
There's no denying it was tough for a while
wandering around with all those feelings in a culture
where feelings were increasingly unwelcome,
where ultimately they were seen as a kind of curse,
where even poets were afraid of words like soul
and pain and spirituality.
                          So, it's good to be dead,
to have given up all claim to being Percy Perfect,
the man whose mind was a series of rooms
graciously opened to an appreciative public;
good to have given up the fruitless quest
for an approval that led right back to the cradle;
good to be shot of the body I was shackled to,
aching to be free, to be some body else.

Of course, being dead has its compensations;
lazing down the years on this yellowing page,
waiting for you to browse your way towards me,
to find me 'accidentally' when we both know
there's really no such thing as an accident.
I feel like the Raven, just three books along,
who waited for the Hero on the road to his doom.
From here you look shiny, young and invulnerable.
Bend closer. Listen. I have something to tell you.

PRAISE SONG TO THE EARTH

Azima wo he, azima wo...
> *Praise chant of the Dagara people*
> *Burkina Faso*

I praise the Earth, still young and rounded,
full and fecund, blowsy in her greening.

I praise the Earth, long-sorrowing mother,
withered, wounded to the point of death
by sons who take the spike to her passivity.

I praise the Earth, awesome and indifferent,
who neither turns nor lashes out but shrugs,
who cannot count, who kills without rancour.

I praise the Earth, her giving and taking,
her generational exchange of life for life,
new flesh for bone, of moistness for aridity.

I praise her but my culture has no words,
no richly polished words of deliciousness
to pour in her honour, to pour like a balm.

I praise the Earth but even here I'm stealing.
These words are my brother's — *Azima Wo.*

VIII

GETTING INTO GREY

A TRAVELLER'S TALE

Well, it finally happened:
I caught myself wearing sandals and socks.
Oh, they were special-import-mountaineering
lightweight-velcro-fastening numbers
but the fact is I was wearing them, voluntarily.
Sandals and socks, there's no excuse.
I'm a wally, a wuss, an ageing hippie.
My hair has opinions; it goes its own way.
I've started dressing like a jumble sale.
Worse, I listen to folk songs — and enjoy them.
It started as a week-end thing
— secretly doing what I used to sneer at —
but now it seems to have bled into my life,
crept up on me, like eating pasta and muesli.
Sometimes I can scarcely believe
that the man in the anorak is actually me,
walking deliberately up a hill
just so that he can walk down the other side;
and the man who stops to smell the hawthorn,
who smiles at strangers and says good morning,
the one who is sad when he hears a sad story,
who wants to go deeper, who doesn't know.
Then I remember another man,
impeccably turned out, booted and suited,
who wore his reserve like a full set of armour,
and I think of the day when, like Sir Parsifal,
he met a band of palmers on the wasted road.
Sir Knight, said the travellers, *what are you doing,*
wearing your armour on a holy day?
The knight errant stopped and looked at himself.
I'm a fool, he said, *I'm a fool*, and he wept.

AFTER THE BEEP

When friends are protected from friendship's call
And machines bar the way like a maid in the hall,
When a click has you gripping the hollow-voiced phone
And your sigh binds the silence that follows the tone,

When the dark in the day and the midsummer chill
Leaves the soul like a vacuum nothing can fill,
When a prayer gives way to an echoing shout
With the knowledge that God, like the others, is out

Then go to the mirror and stare at the face
And study each line and the pain and the grace,
Then know that the face and the eyes and the heart
Are all that you have. It's enough — make a start.

TO A TALENTED YOUNG FRIEND

For J. V.

Take a walk in the woods. Follow any path.
Slip your city shoes off and feel the mud
oozing between your shocked, wet toes.
Get messy, get lost, get rat-arsed if you need to,
but remember to allow the daemon beside you
to whisper his charm when you step out on the ledge.
Take care to squander your years effectively.
Enjoy the moment, the tingle and the rush;
and when the Grail Castle opens its secretive door
to offer you a kingdom for a question answered,
don't worry if you stumble, or get it wrong —
wrong is the right thing to be doing right now.
The Wasteland will come with its tears and cinders,
its shaming Damoselles, and confining armour.
For the moment feel the wind as it rakes your skin,
calls on you to make that first incredible leap.
Trust it. Lean on it. You're a young hawk. Fly.

TEARAWAY

Above the falls it looks so easy.
The trickle from your soggy field
is an invitation to the world,
while the brook that runs from this beginning
is clear curiosity, a promise of adventure.
It draws you like a tender leaf;
new-fallen, floating; already separate.

The growing pull brings on the shallows:
movement, noise and fast-cut images;
sudden tunnels of hurried green, made loud
by the gathering of talkative waters;
bends that open onto dazzling reaches
of rippling spill and wordless chatter.

Ahead of you, you wouldn't know it
from the passing banks and nodding reeds,
something awaits you, something unthinking,
slow and pike-like, of sinuous cruelty.
In the calm, your reflection smiles up at you.
You shatter it with a casual hand.
The water lifts you, carries you forward.

UP FROM HAIGHT ASHBURY

He finally gets to San Francisco

The raven sits on the arm of a lamppost,
his croak distinct in the piney air.
He's watching a hopelessness of dossers,
gathering, blinking, scratching their arses
as they climb out of their cardboard barrio
just by the entrance to Golden Gate Park.

The raven sharpens his beak on the metalwork,
tapping out a warning from the Other World.
You'd expect the dossers here to be old hippies —
washed-out tattoos and toothless chucklings,
but they are all young — American innocents,
blown in from Idaho and the lonely Dakotas.

I'm in mid-swerve, and turning to leave
in my just-been-clocked-by-a-crack-dealer way,
when I realise that this is what I was here for,
a glimpse of my yearned-for-yet-unlived youth.
The crack dealer smiles, and promptly forgets me.
The raven follows me all the way home.

MORNINGS

I love these mornings, these do-nothing mornings:
the old house, still, accepting, idling;
jackdaws squabbling around the chimney tops
while a robin rehearses on the quince;
the slow light, warming the tired stone,
and the nearby bleat of March-born lambs.

Windy mornings too — their shallow bluster,
their wheedling question, and complaint:
the casements rattling, the fluttering glass,
the whole house protesting, talking to itself:
resentful draughts, shrill and needy,
the angry slam of a put-upon door.

And those other mornings, like a shapeless prayer,
mumbled, incoherent, yet of infinite solace:
the settling-in of a day-long drizzle,
the amplified drip of air-become-water —
stasis, surrender, saturation —
gathered and gentled by the constant rain.

MEMENTO

On my wall I have a stone, a remnant
which I liberated from a public park,
from a midden littered with empty cans,
discarded bottles and foul-smelling rubbish.
It's the shoulder of a broken gravestone,
a smashed-off wedge from a limestone truckle.
It boasts a single, barely recognisable face
of careful lettering that says no more than

           IN MEM...
and
           FRANCES...
           WHO DEPAR...
and then
        ... YEARS...

I know little about it, except that the park
was once the graveyard of a debtor's prison,
home to the frivolous and the impecunious.
I saved it one damp and wintry morning
after I'd seen it hurled by a wino who screamed
like Moses throwing down the Tablets,
red-faced, indignant, inspired in his rage.
I got it home and hosed it down, scraped it
then scrubbed it, then left it in a tub of bleach.
I wanted, or rather I needed, to make it clean.
Now it's a memorial to my own prodigal dead:
the bellicose lads and the sad inebriate women,
the blowsy wives and their bitter defeated men.
At times I can almost smell the tap-rooms,
with their fug of yeast and rough-cut tobacco.
I imagine the faces, determined and cheerful,
three-sheets-to-the-wind or melancholy-sour.

I see the bravery, the fear, the constant striving,
the recurring failure and the turning-away.

On my wall, a fragment of broken headstone
to remind me of people who are all but forgotten.
Sometimes I can sit and ponder it, fondly;
at other times, I still need to scrub it clean.

BAD DAY

I'm watching bluebells nodding in the orchard
when I think of my father for the first time in years.
A breeze of grief stirs the damson blossom
then dances away among the trees.

If there's a measure for us, it's our parents,
and in those terms I haven't done too badly:
real love, a home, some genuine friendships —
but I would have liked a body of work, something
for the memory to run its fingers over,
something to leave with a chance of lasting.

I can't count the projects I've left unfinished,
dumped because of a negative word
that carried the edge of my parents' contempt.

What I wanted, what I lacked, was a sense of blessing.
What I got was the acid burning of their scorn.
And now I'm angry. It's the same old pattern:
first grief, then shame, then ruinous anger.

The buzzards have left their nest down the lane.
They circle over the house, rising on a thermal.

I'm looking at sixty, and still having bad days.
Sometimes you just want to fly away.

THREE RAGAS

(i)

Morning

The music comes to me,
drifting over the lake,
as a breeze strokes the face
of the smoky waters.

I am eating the air of India
but I am a coach-party wallah
and very young. My English shoes
have barely stirred the dust.

The music speaks of Siva
the Destroyer and his Sakti
though I am blind to him
dancing in his circle of fire.

As for Kali, the Smiling One
with her terrible necklace,
I have no patience to sit
with her and count the skulls.

The ache in my body says,
Stay. Sit and listen,
but my head says. *Look!*
Over there, an elephant!

I'm off down the road again.
The music fades behind me.
My shoes keep their polish
in spite of the dust.

THREE RAGAS

(ii)

Afternoon

The Delhi kites are circling
and a fever is upon me
as my rickshaw threads
its way against the flow.

On a time-out from business
thirty years later
I'm staring at some pi-dogs
as they squabble for scraps.

One noses something
that catches my eye – a man
laid out upon the ground
in a strange and listless pose.

He's lying in a clearing
left by the multitude
that eddies around him
on its way to the Mosque.

This man is no drunkard.
This man is no junkie.
This man is dying,
alone, on the pavement.

I look back, a sick, fat man
on a rickshaw. Our dull eyes
meet for a moment,
then he covers his face.

THREE RAGAS

(iii)

Evening

In the City of Ghats
overlooking Mother Ganga
Siva is dancing
as the pyres crackle and spit.

I am lying on a day bed
humouring a doctor
as a lizard smiles above me:
Kali waiting for lunch.

The doctor is a kindly soul
but he doesn't know
what's wrong. I am weak.
He is sweet. I am afraid.

Below on a mud bank
a herdsman beats a buffalo.
The whack of his lathi
offends the sandalwood air.

Outside in the alleyway
someone is chanting.
I'm held by it, ambushed,
taken by surprise.

My journeyed heart begins
to open. I am by a lake,
enchanted by an older music,
dusty – ready to hear.

FOUND WANTING

Late afternoon in early April,
a wisp of cloud in a clear blue sky.
The scent of balsam is sweetening the air
while the greens of young larch, willow, and hazel
combine to form the first rush of spring.
I'm watching the buzzards cruising their territories,
cadging an updraft to the lip of the cwm,
where they hover to note the scavenging options:
a wounded roebuck, a stillborn lamb, a rabbit
too far from the safety of the warren.
They circle languidly back to the edge again,
lazing on a thermal, waiting for a death.

Watching them, I think of my cousin Anne.
A natural connection, she just soars into my mind,
and hangs there the way the dead sometimes do.
I felt ashamed when she died, having failed to find her
when she lay dying, and I was in the area.
We write, we call – make the minimum effort –
but the news of a death still leaves us judged.
Prepare to feel guilty, she said to me once
when we were anticipating the deaths of our mothers.

I wish she had come here, had stayed in this house.
I wanted her to see me settled at last, to be witness
to my landing, my joy and good fortune.
But it wasn't to happen, we didn't reconnect,
so a part of me will stay the callow nonentity
she would have considered me right up to the end.

It's going to be a beautiful evening.
Things are gathering for the little revelation
that often occurs here, around this time. The alders still
and begin to darken as the shadows of the hanger
pour like honey and the larches point towards the indigo.
Everything waits for the evening star.

OTHERWISE

It could have been otherwise. The world
might have been baked a different shape.
We could have been sovereigns, or simple
saints, lovers of earth or seaborne wanderers.
But no, we are ourselves and torn between
the need for love and what we call our duty.
Life can be cruel, has never been otherwise,
so we have learned some iron truths:
that hardships lead to a hardness in the heart
and that work often serves in place of love.
But on a rolling blue afternoon in April
we can sit and watch the world unwinding,
remembering the light as well as the darkness,
and see ourselves for what we really are:
plain people, good, for all we feel otherwise,
gifted with a talent for thought and kindness.
That's when we gently reopen to the world,
to the drifting blossom and the scent of lilac.
It's another spring. The world has survived.
Life has a beauty and — admit it — so do we.

AN AFTERWORD:

THE INHERITANCE AND THE UNDERWORLD

These poems were not originally written with a collection in mind. Over a period of nearly twenty years they have spoken to live audiences: affirming, comforting and occasionally enlightening people about their own struggles and obsessions. They were written to be spoken, often with specific groups and gatherings in mind. As such they were put to work – in the room – and so served their purpose.

They have rarely been published, either because of sheer laziness on my part or because they don't fit into the current mold of what poetry ought to be. Though I would have liked it to be otherwise, they have been variously dismissed as "straightforward", "uncomplicated" or downright "simple". From a high literary point of view then, they may not be great literature, but from the point of view of an audience member who distrusts poetry – who may have felt belittled or shunned by it in its modern dress – they are clear, direct, and accessible. Together, they chart a journey from a largely unconscious and wounded victimhood to a hard-won, if still partial, self-awareness and acceptance. They change over the years in quality, density and focus, reflecting developments in character and style. It's uneven and occasionally rough stuff but it's honest, and of its moment, and as such I decided to hang it together as a sequence or collection, rather than jettison parts of it as a form of juvenilia or 'therapeutic poetry' (such a contemptuous phrase).

In fact, the underworld journey this collection points to did involve numerous therapies, both psychotherapeutic and physical. There were also innumerable workshops and seminars, men's groups and gatherings, initiatory rituals, retreats and shamanic explorations. The poems reflect this eclectic mix of influences in their assorted styles and responses. Over time, some did get published in magazines while others lay in drawers until they were dusted off and brought out for the readings and events, which evolved out of my work.

I have acknowledged individual publishers and thanked my teachers and guides elsewhere, but I would also like to acknowledge the men and women who shared this journey and allowed me to join them in their own particular versions of the underworld. Though many of them remain un-named, and occasionally anonymous, that doesn't mean they have been overlooked or forgotten. We all have an inheritance and many of us struggle to speak our truth. Some never get to say a word, still less receive a hearing. This book charts one journey from silence to self-expression – sometimes just speaking is a victory.

William Ayot
Mathern
2011

INDEX OF FIRST LINES

Like this, like a revelation, here and now, 102
Love me she said, opening to him like a well 88
Maria has been shamed so many times 46
Much thinner than he ought to be, 15
My father doesn't haunt me anymore. 40
My mother doesn't really know me. 74
My son, there are things you need to know, 38
Night after night the empty road, 96
Not the mourners with their drizzled faces, 20
On my wall I have a stone, a remnant 112
Oooh Lovely! 90
Pheasants on a branch 100
Salt Woman, hidden in a world of tears, 91
Someone once explained to me, patiently, 68
Sunday was my father's birthday. 42
Take a walk in the woods. Follow any path. 108
The beauty of men lies in the doing: 64
The Delhi kites are circling 116
The fist came out of nowhere. 23
The Grandmothers hover in the spaces 75
The grief came up unbidden, like water 36
The kilderkins lying in the cool of the cellar 24
The music comes to me, 115
The night my father died 31
The raven sits on the arm of a lamppost, 110
The years have all vanished like old Slindon Wood. 19
They used to come to her at night, the nine-year-olds, 28
This evening, for a while, 76
This is the fear 16
Today my hands 34
Tonight the stars are broken glass. 82
Two o'clock in the morning and the moon 29
Wanting to say something to his mother; 65
Was it Sue? Forgive me, I've forgotten her name 80
We are standing together, my long-lost brother and I, 62
We sat awhile and contemplated the departing river 63
We're going to see 101
Well, it finally happened: 106
What's all the shouting about? 78
When friends are protected from friendship's call 107
Who's that? What an extraordinary face. 81
Why do the young lads bellow in the park 58
Year's end, and the grief is with me, 12
You go back to the numbers, 27
You see something behind their eyes, 45

 **PS AVALON PUBLISHING**

About PS Avalon

PS Avalon Publishing is an independent and committed publisher offering a complete publishing service. As a small publisher able to take advantage of the latest technological advances, PS Avalon Publishing can offer an alternative route for aspiring authors in our particular fields of interest.

As well as publishing, we offer an education programme including courses, seminars, group retreats, and other opportunities for personal and spiritual growth. Whilst the nature of our work means we engage with people from all around the world, we are based in Glastonbury which is in the West Country of England.

new poetry books

Our purpose is to bring you the best new poetry with a psychospiritual content, work that is contemplative and inspirational, with a dark, challenging edge.

self development books

We publish inspiring reading material aimed at enhancing your personal and spiritual development in which everything is kept as simple and as accessible as possible.

PS AVALON PUBLISHING

Box 1865, Glastonbury,

Somerset BA6 8YR, U.K.

www.willparfitt.com

will@willparfitt.com